10-Minute Scrapbook Pages

Hundreds of Easy, Innovative Designs

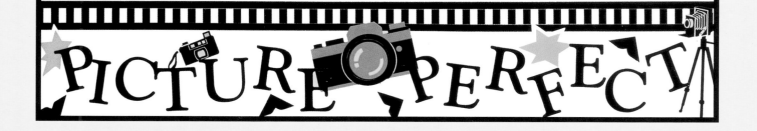

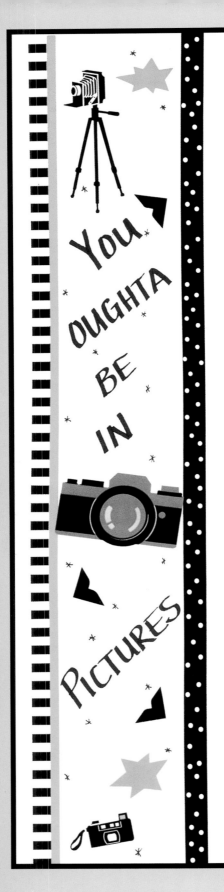

You
OUGHTA
BE
IN
Pictures

10-Minute Scrapbook Pages

Hundreds of Easy, Innovative Designs

Raquel Boehme

Sterling Publishing Co., Inc. New York
A Sterling / Chapelle Book

Chapelle:

Jo Packham, Owner

Cathy Sexton, Editor

Staff: Marie Barber, Ann Bear, Areta Bingham, Kass Burchett, Rebecca Christensen, Brenda Doncouse, Dana Durney, Marilyn Goff, Holly Hollingsworth, Susan Jorgensen, Barbara Milburn, Linda Orton, Karmen Quinney, Leslie Ridenour, Cindy Stoeckl, Gina Swapp

Designers: Linda Aarhus, Lisa Arnold, Lisa Barber, Raquel Boehme, Annette Brandley, Madelyn Brownell, Lisa Farmer, Lauretta Hill, Robin Kruger, Jennifer Newhouse, Nancy Ray, Judith Sehlmeier, LeeAnn Wentz, and Tammy Westbroek

Photographic images on pages 2, 6–7, 16–18, 20–26, 29, 31, 37, 47–48, 55, 59, 61, 63, 67–68, 73, 75, 81, 87, 90, 108–109, 117, 120–121, and 123 are © Copyright 1996–1999 PhotoDisc, Inc. All rights reserved.

If you have any questions or comments or would like information on specialty products featured in this book, please contact Chapelle, Ltd., Inc., P.O. Box 9252, Ogden, UT 84409 • (801) 621-2777 • (801) 621-2788 Fax • e-mail: chapelle@chapelleltd.com

Library of Congress Cataloging-in-Publication Data
    Boehme, Raquel.
        10-minute scrapbook pages : hundreds of easy innovative designs / Raquel Boehme.
            p.   cm.
        "A Sterling/Chapelle book."
        Includes index.
        ISBN 0-8069-1971-X
         1. Photograph albums. 2. Photographs--Conservation and restoration. 3. Scrapbooks.
      I. Title: Ten minute scrapbook pages. II. Title
    TR465.B64 2000   99-049670
    745.593--dc21   CIP

10 9 8 7 6 5 4

First paperback edition published 2001 by
Sterling Publishing Company, Inc.
387 Park Avenue South, New York, NY 10016
© 2000 by Chapelle Ltd.
Distributed in Canada by Sterling Publishing
c/o Canadian Manda Group, One Atlantic Avenue, Suite 105
Toronto, Ontario, Canada M6K 3E7
Distributed in Great Britain by Chrysalis Books
64 Brewery Road, London N7 9NT, England
Distributed in Australia by Capricorn Link (Australia) Pty. Ltd.
P.O. Box 704, Windsor, NSW 2756 Australia
Printed in China
All Rights Reserved

Sterling ISBN 0-8069-1971-X Trade
            0-8069-1780-6 Paper

MY HERITAGE

About the author

Raquel Redford Boehme was raised in Orem, Utah. She currently resides in Pleasant View, Utah, with her husband, Scott, and her three children, Ashlie, Taylor, and Nathan.

Raquel has a Bachelor of Science degree in Family and Consumer Sciences from Utah State University. She has taught in the public schools and is now the owner/director of her own preschool.

She has worked in the photo album industry for the past six years as a Creative Memories consultant and leader. She has received numerous awards including the company's "Spirit of Success" award.

Dedication

To my scrapbooking friends who help inspire, teach, create, and share the never-ending value of such an important work—preserving family heritage.

Acknowledgments

I would like to acknowledge the support of my husband who understands my need to create and to help others through the process of storing and documenting their precious family memories. I would also like to thank my children who enthusiastically open their books and look through the pages—what better thanks than to know your work is appreciated and enjoyed.

Thanks to my mom, I have been a scrapbooker all my life. As I teach classes and hold scrapbooking workshops, I see the need for a simple approach to scrapbooking, because not all of us are equipped with the creativity nor the time to make each page a "work of art." I hope you will enjoy the simple creativity of the timesaving border ideas. After all, I believe the goal is to have completed albums, not another unfinished project.

Contents

Family Fun 68

Holidays & Seasons 90

Vacation 78

No Season No Reason 123

The Basics

Introduction

Scrapbooking is a rewarding activity that can be enjoyed by people of any age. In addition to being a lot of fun, scrapbooking promotes a strong sense of belonging and self-esteem. This book was designed to offer hundreds of easy, innovative designs for scrapbook pages that can be created in just ten minutes.

When you put time and effort into creating scrapbook pages, you want to make certain they will last for many years. Therefore, archival products should be used. One of the culprits for deteriorating pages is acid. Over time, acid will eat away at anything it comes in contact with, causing it to become yellow and brittle. When using acid-free, photo-safe products, you eliminate this risk.

On occasion you may want to include items that are not acid-free, such as certificates or greeting cards. These items can be included, but should be kept from touching any other item. Placing them in a page protector by themselves is one option; another would be to spray the items with a buffer spray which will neutralize the pH levels.

Choosing an album

Photo albums come in a variety of styles, sizes, and colors. Find an album that suits your personality and style.

The most important function of an album is to make certain the binding allows the scrapbook pages to be protected on all sides and that the pages are able to lay flat.

The main differences between albums are their size and their binding. Albums are available in a variety of sizes, but the two most popular sizes are: $8^1/_2$" x 11" and 12" x 12". The most popular album bindings allow the album to expand and give the flexibility of removing or adding pages.

When choosing the perfect albums to be used for your scrapbooks, you may opt to use several different sizes. Think about whether you want all of your scrapbooks to match or whether you prefer them all to be different.

Gathering supplies

• <u>Acid-free paper or card stock</u> should be used as the background for your scrapbook page. All embellishments can be adhered to it with a photo-safe adhesive
of your choice. When creating scrapbook pages with borders made from die-cuts or stickers, white paper or card stock is the most commonly used.

Acid-free paper or card stock is available in several colors, patterns, and textures. This gives a wonderful variety for matting your photographs, making die-cuts, or using craft punches.

• <u>Adhesives</u> should be chosen according to personal preference. Double-sided tape is the most popular when adhering your photographs onto your scrapbook pages. Photo-safe adhesive pens, made for scrapbooking, allow you to apply the precise amount of adhesive to small areas of die-cuts or silhouetted photographs. Spray adhesive that has been specially designed for adhering photographs onto scrapbook pages is also quite popular.

• <u>Permanent markers</u> are used for highlighting, decorating, and journaling. A fine-point marker works best for fine lines, tiny accents, and journaling. Medium-point and calligraphy markers work best for adding titles to your scrapbook pages.

Using a variety of colored markers adds interest to your pages.

• A "<u>red eye</u>" pen is used to remove the red from the eyes of people and animals in some photographs, which is caused by the flash.

• A photo-safe, <u>soft art pencil</u> is used to trace the shape from a template onto your photograph. Once the photograph has been cut into the traced shape, the excess pencil can be wiped away with a soft cloth without damaging the photograph.

• <u>Scissors</u> are essential. A large pair of craft scissors works well for basic cutting, while a small pair makes detailed cutting much easier.

• A sharp <u>craft knife</u> with replaceable blades can be helpful when cutting straight edges and tight corners.

It is also a useful tool for removing stickers that have been temporarily placed on your background paper or card stock.

• A <u>paper trimmer</u> is used for trimming strips of paper or card stock, but most often it is used for cropping photographs. Because it has a straight edge, photos can be cropped very easily with great precision.

• <u>Decorative scissors</u> are available in several designs and are a fun way to accent your photo matting.

Keep in mind that most pairs of decorative scissors will cut two patterns depending on the direction you hold them while cutting.

• <u>Page protectors</u> serve the most important function of all. They protect your finished scrapbook pages. They are available in lightweight, medium-weight, heavy-weight, and super heavy-weight and are available with a clear or a nonglare finish. Keep in mind that your page protectors should be archival quality.

• <u>Templates</u> are plastic patterns for cutting basic shapes and simple designs. Using a grease pencil, trace the shape from any template onto your photograph or selected paper or card stock. Then cut around the traced line so your cut piece will be the shape of the template design.

• <u>Die-cuts</u> are precut shapes of images that have been cut from acid-free paper or card stock. Most of these images are simple images that can be used alone or layered to add more color and detail.

- <u>Stickers</u> are simple to use and are a fun way to decorate any scrapbook page. Sticker collecting has been popular for decades and scrapbook enthusiasts have found a great way to put those stickers to use. Long sticker strips can be used to border or divide a page, while smaller stickers can be used to fill in or accent a decorative theme.

If you are unsure if a sticker is photo-safe, check the labeling. Recently manufactured stickers will be labeled; older stickers may not be. When in doubt, do not use.

- <u>Rulers</u> are essential for marking strips of paper or card stock and photographs that need to be cut straight. They are also used to draw straight rules when creating borders on your scrapbook pages.

Decorative rulers come in a variety of styles and allow wonderful options for enhancing borders.

Taking photographs

Great scrapbooks start with great photographs. Although professional photographs are a wonderful addition to any scrapbook, personal snapshots capture unforgettable moments. The more scrapbooking you do, the better your photography will become. The reason is because you will become tuned-in to the subject matter and will eventually learn to crop out unnecessary backgrounds.

Photographs of children are often better when taken on a child's level. Do not be afraid to try new angles and take more than one shot of your subject. If your camera has a "zoom" feature, use it to capture intimate details and priceless expressions.

Have your film developed at a reputable film laboratory to ensure the best possible color and quality of processing paper. In addition, get double prints. They are generally inexpensive when requested at the same time as the original film processing.

Cropping photographs

Cropping photographs will enhance them and can make the subject(s) appear closer or larger. Many times a photograph has too much background or foreground and cropping allows you to remove unwanted areas.

Cropping photographs is completely optional. Some scrapbookers are not comfortable with this process and that is okay. If you choose to crop your photos, make certain to use a paper trimmer to ensure straight lines.

Cropping is a completely safe technique, but it is irreversible. If you need to crop an irreplaceable, one-of-a-kind photograph, consider making and

cropping a color copy of it. Also, instant photos should not be cropped because of the chemicals inside them.

Photographs can be cropped into any shape from a template. A soft art pencil is used to trace the shape onto your photograph. Once the photograph has been cut into the traced shape, the excess pencil can be wiped away with a soft cloth without damaging the photograph.

Templates are available in hundreds of designs and themes. Keep in mind that cookie cutters make great templates.

Circle and oval cutters are also available. If you choose to crop several of your photographs into circles or ovals, these tools will save you a lot of time.

Silhouetting a photograph is another option. This simply means trimming around the subject in a photograph, following its contours. This technique is not for every page or photograph, but sometimes silhouetting enhances the page and/or the photograph and enables you to place more photographs on a page.

When silhouetting a photograph, use a small pair of scissors so you can cut around corners and delicate areas. Take extra care when cutting around "hair" to ensure that heads are not misshapen!

Matting photographs

Once your photographs are cropped as desired, matting them is simple. Photographs may look better when they are surrounded by "a little bit of color or decoration." Selective matting may accent your photograph and enhance your entire scrapbook page.

Select an acid-free paper or card stock that is complementary to your photograph. Small patterned papers, as well as solid papers, make attractive mats.

Using the photo-safe adhesive of your choice, adhere the photographs to the paper or card stock. Trim around the photograph with a trimmer or decorative scissors to leave a mat of the desired width — from $1/8$" to $1/2$" are most common. Wider mats are nice for larger photographs. When double- or triple-matting a photograph, the outer mat is generally wider than the inner mat(s).

Precut mats are available and make an attractive accent to most photographs.

Journaling

Journaling is the term used for documenting the "who, what, when, where, and why" of each photograph or for each group of photographs. The journaling will help explain a subject or record an event more clearly. It should be done with a permanent marker (also referred to as a journaling pen or marker). In addition, your personal handwriting adds "a part of you" to your scrapbook creations.

Writing personal feelings and adding captions about the subject(s) gives scrapbook pages added value and interest. Include family stories, traditions, poems, and songs that correspond with the photographs. A child's first words or favorite phrase enhances priceless photographs.

Creative lettering is a way of decorating and accenting scrapbook pages. The decorative text becomes an element of the page design, drawing attention to the words as well as the photographs.

There are several books available to give you ideas. Experiment on scratch paper and come up with your own unique style. Until you are comfortable, you may want to write the title or lettering on the page with pencil, then go over the pencil with a permanent marker.

Alphabet stickers can also be used for labeling purposes. Fun phrases or messages can be added with letter and number stickers.

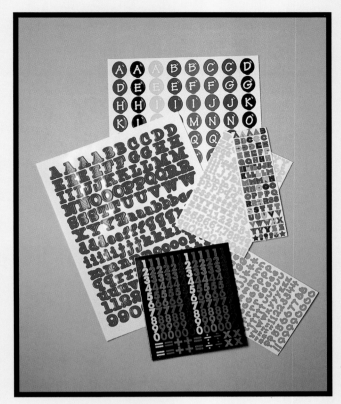

Several alphabet lettering styles in a variety of sizes are available and can be used separately or mixed with other colors and/or styles to add dimension and interest.

Using die-cuts

Using die-cuts to embellish scrapbook pages is easy and inexpensive. Because die-cuts are precut shapes of images that have been cut from acid-free paper or card stock, generally they are used alone. When additional color and detail is desired, die-cuts can be layered.

Position the die-cuts as desired. Using the photo-safe adhesive of your choice, adhere the die-cuts to the background paper or card stock.

Here is an example of several die-cuts that have been positioned and layered for an eye-catching vertical border on the right-hand side of the scrapbook page.

CLOWNIN' AROUND

Die-cuts can be used in untraditional ways as well. Here, three ice-cream cone die-cuts have been turned upside down and used as clowns.

The addition of stickers helps accent the clown faces, as well as the entire scrapbook page.

Using stickers

Using photo-safe stickers to embellish scrapbook pages is simple and is a fun way to carry out a specific theme. Long, page-length stickers may be used to create a border along the edge of a page.

Stickers should be adhesive-backed. Carefully arrange the stickers on the background paper or card stock as desired without applying too much pressure to each sticker. This makes it simple to remove the sticker for repositioning when necessary. A sharp craft knife is a useful tool for removing stickers that have been temporarily placed on your background paper or card stock.

Once the design is in place, press each sticker on the background paper or card stock with clean hands.

If stickers need to be removed permanently or temporarily for repositioning, a commercial adhesive stabi-lizer can be used so that no damage is done to the background paper or card stock or to other stickers that have been used. Once the sticker(s) has been removed, it can be reused by repositioning it and pressing it into its new position.

Stickers, when layered, can add dimension. When possible, and if desired, place one sticker slightly over another or "weave" one in and out of another similar to the way the ribbons and letters have been layered on the scrapbook page shown above.

Here is an example of stickers that have been layered. The teddy bear was first placed on the background page. The birthday cake was placed on top of the teddy bear and the letter "B" on top of the cake. The chef's hat, wooden spoon, and rolling pin were also placed on top of the teddy bear. A permanent marker was then used to add the nursery rhyme to complete the scrapbook page.

Pat-a-cake pat-a-cake Baker's man Bake me a cake as fast as you can. pit it and pat it and mark it with "B" and . . . throw it in the oven for baby and me!

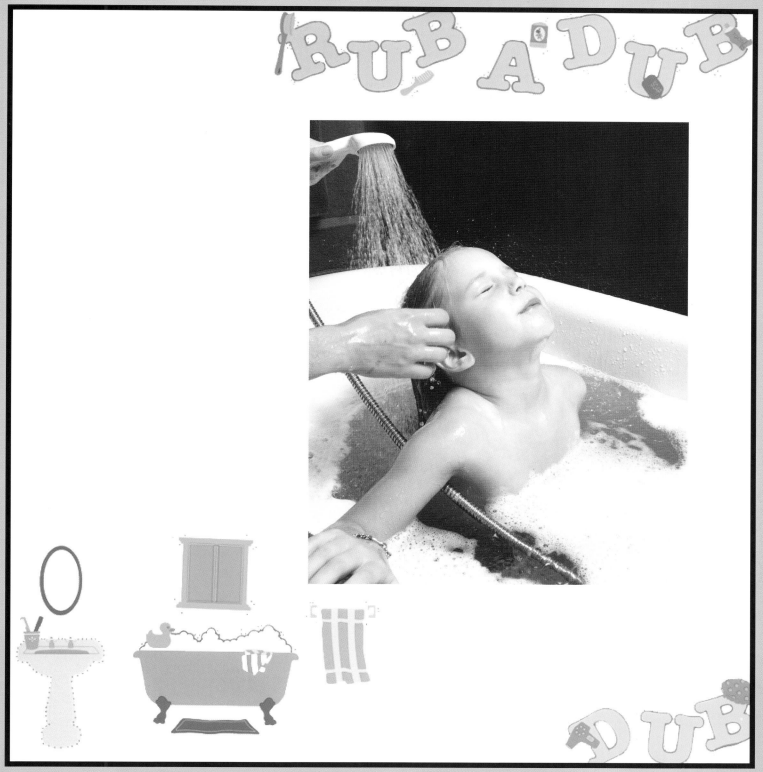

Here is an example of how permanent markers are often used to help accent stickers. The letter stickers have been outlined with the marker to add contrast as well as to help draw attention to each letter. Tiny accent dots also have been randomly added around each letter to add interest to the scrapbook page.

'Twas the night before Christmas, 🎄 When all through the house 🍪 Not a creature was stirring, ❤️ not even a mouse; 🔔 The stockings were hung by the chimney with care 🎀 in hopes that St. Nicholas soon would be there.

Here is an example of using stickers in an untraditional way. The small stickers, all with a common theme, have been used to separate text where a natural break or pause should be.

To finish the scrapbook page, a cluster of layered stickers has been added in the lower right-hand corner.

22

Using rulers and decorative rulers

When creating borders for your scrapbook pages, a ruler is an important tool. Straight lines can be drawn by placing the ruler in the desired position, then drawing the line with a permanent marker. The effect the rule or line will have on the scrapbook page will depend on the color and size of the marker tip.

Decorative rulers are great because of the variety of styles that is available —from wavy to scallop, from zigzag to victorian. The versatility of borders that can be created with decorative rulers is literally unlimited. When using rulers, it is recommended that the border be placed on the scrapbook page first and then embellished.

Here is an example of a single line drawn with a medium-point permanent black marker, then accented with a single wavy line drawn with a fine-point permanent black marker. Stickers were used to embellish the tops of both lines, then additional letter stickers were used to title the scrapbook page.

A decorative ruler with a scallop design was used to make the first vertical and horizontal lines (pink). Second vertical and horizontal lines were then positioned and drawn (green).

Accent marks to resemble "watermelon seeds" were made with a permanent black marker. Stickers were then added to accent the lower left-hand corner of the scrapbook page.

This scrapbook page was created by overlapping heart stickers in small clusters. Then, two fine-point permanent markers in complementary colors were used to add accent around and between each heart cluster. Such simple detailing can add so much to the overall look and feel of your scrapbook page.

Oh Baby!

What was used:
- Stickers
- Strip of card stock

What was used:
- Die-cuts
- Stickers

What was used:
- Die-cuts
- Stickers

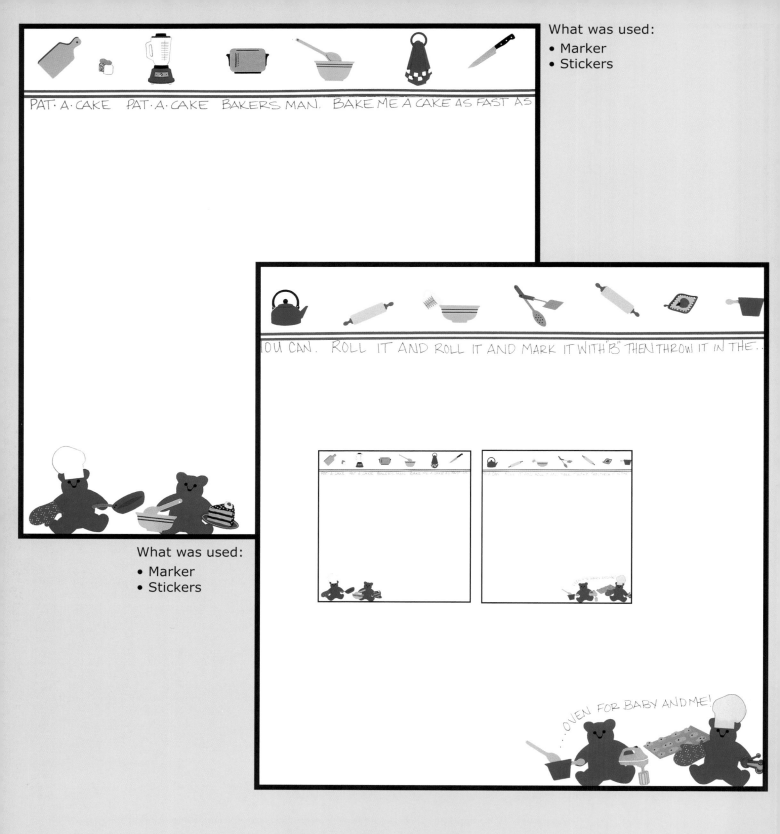

Rub-a-dub dub three men in a tub...

a butcher... a baker... a candlestick maker.

What was used:
- Die-cut
- Marker
- Stickers

What was used:
- Decorative ruler
- Markers
- Stickers

SWEET LIL' THINGS

What was used:
- Markers
- Ruler
- Stickers

30

SOME BUNNY SPECIAL

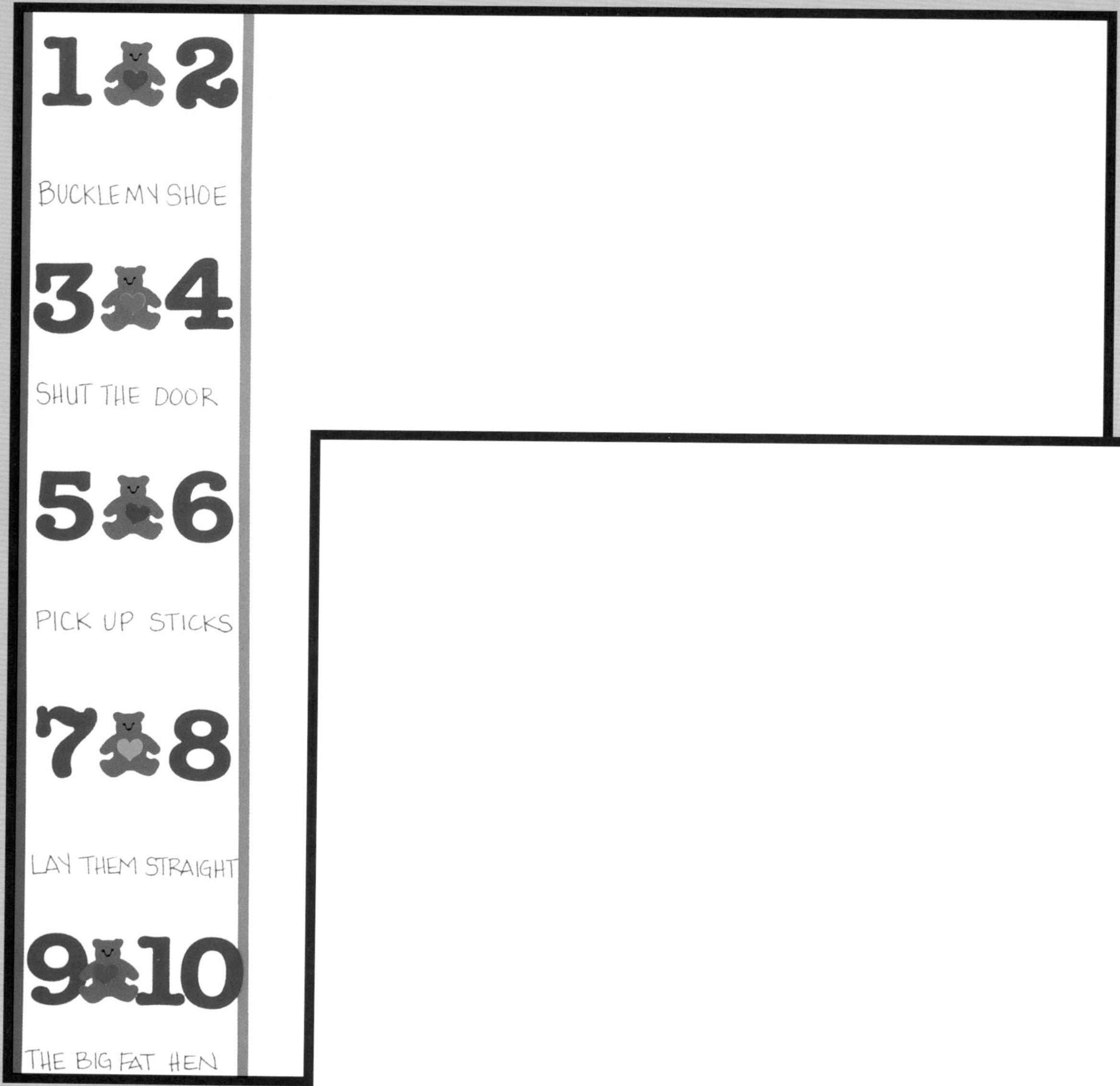

1 2

BUCKLE MY SHOE

3 4

SHUT THE DOOR

5 6

PICK UP STICKS

7 8

LAY THEM STRAIGHT

9 10

THE BIG FAT HEN

What was used:
• Markers
• Ruler
• Stickers

What was used:
• Marker
• Stickers

SEE HOW THEY GROW

What was used:
- Markers
- Ruler
- Stickers

What was used:
- Die-cuts
- Markers
- Ruler
- Stickers

Our Family

Stitched with Love

34

two·by·two·by·two·

CHICKEN POX

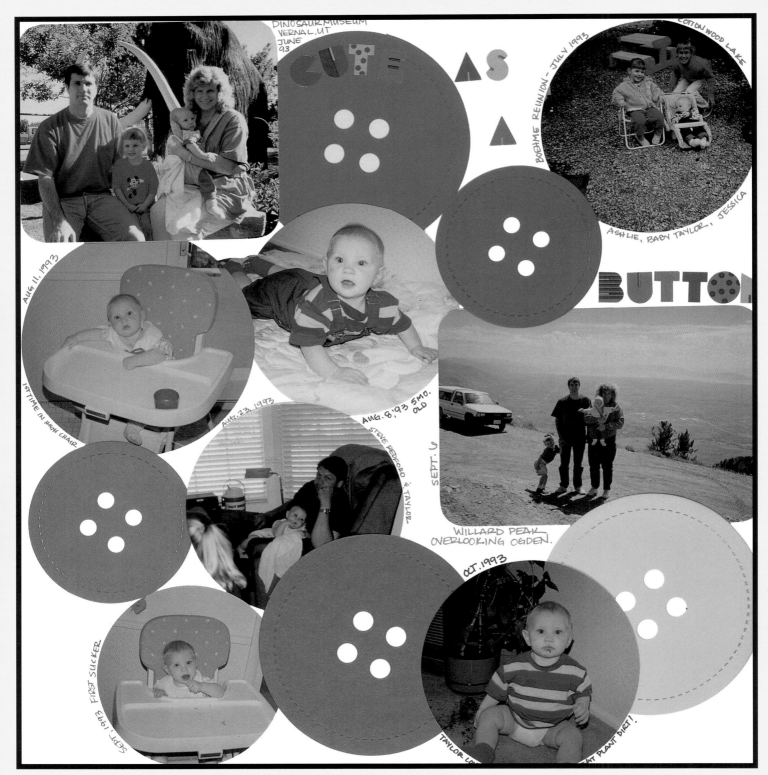

DINOSAUR MUSEUM VERNAL, UT JUNE 93

COTTONWOOD LAKE

CUTE AS A

BOEHME REUNION - JULY 1993

ASHLIE, BABY TAYLOR, JESSICA

BUTTON

AUG 11, 1993

1ST TIME IN HIGH CHAIR.

AUG. 23, 1993

AUG. 8, '93 5 MO. OLD

STEVE REDFORD & TAYLOR

SEPT. 6

WILLARD PEAK, OVERLOOKING OGDEN.

OCT. 1993

SEPT. 1993 FIRST SUCKER

TAYLOR

EAT PLANT DIRT!

What was used:
- Die-cuts
- Markers
- Stickers

4 to 5 yr. old class

(mom)
Mrs. Raquel
Tyler Davies
Jake Hatch
Devin Flora
Alexis Koontz
ReAnna Madsen
Charlee Smith
Laina Call
Taylor Boehme
Heather McArtor
Sarah Tidwell
Marissa
Michael Jamison

Preschool Certificate

Raquel's Little Extras Preschool

Congratulations

Taylor Boehme

You have completed Preschool and are awarded this Certificate in recognition of your accomplishments.

Proudly presented from Raquel's Little Extras Preschool on this date, May 21, 1996

by *Mom*

What was used:
• Markers
• Stickers

SCHOOL

School is Cool !! School is Cool !! School is

ASHLIE IN MRS. BRINTON'S FIRST GRADE CLASS

ASHLIE BOEHME   MAY 1997

3+4=7

1-1=0

Kathy Brinton
First Grade

Lomond View Elementary
1996-1997

Val Parrish
Principal

TOP ROW: Mr. Parrish, Angela Larson, Samantha Rawson, Eric Schmidt, Heather Raitt, Cole Eckhardt, Jordan Ballif, Bradley Ferguson, Tyler McDonald **ROW 2:** Chanel Carlile, Aaron Hoskins, Cole Charlton, Sean Marsden, Jonathon Burnett, Cami Carlile, Tori Moran, Ms. Brinton **BOTTOM ROW:** D. J. North, Karen Montgomery, Ben Feller, Jessica Ritchie, Hillary Jensen, Whitney Smith, Ashlie Boehme, Mekenzie Ross, Joshua Clementz

What was used:

- Marker
- Ruler
- Stickers

May 1996

Trout farm with Dad And the young men's Group from our ward.

Taylor Boehme

3-4 yr old class

Mrs. Raquel

Skyler Jackson

Tyler Anderson

Taylor Boehme

Clayson Cook

James Neeley

Aaron Hall

Makenzy Turner

Valerie Braegger

Sierra Sorensen

Andrew Hall

Little Extras Preschool

What was used:
- Decorative ruler
- Markers
- Ruler
- Stickers

42

Ashlie's Artwork

What was used:
• Markers
• Ruler
• Stickers

What was used:
- Marker
- Stickers

What was used:
- Die-cuts
- Stickers

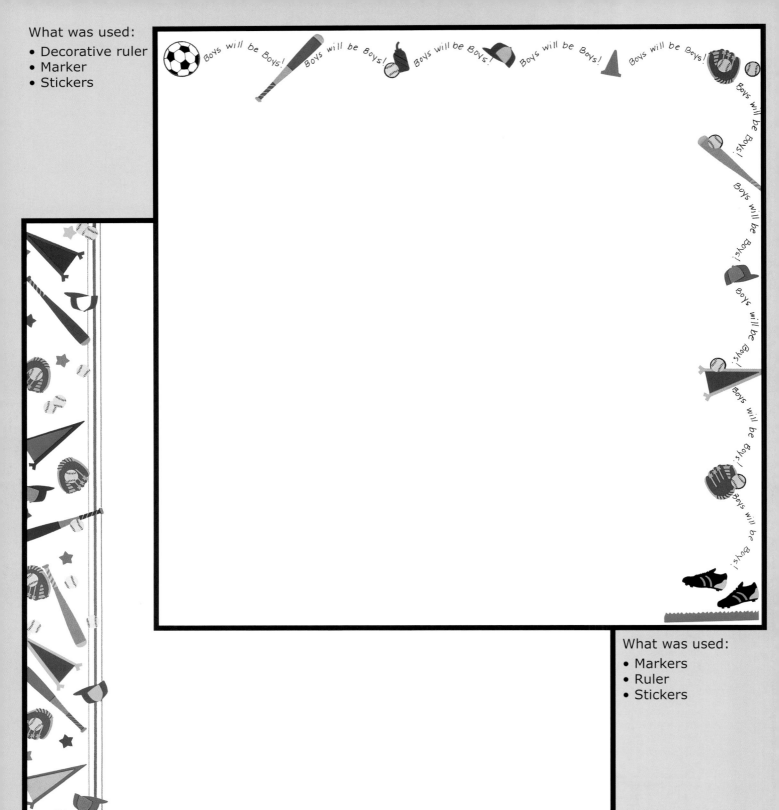

What was used:
- Decorative ruler
- Marker
- Stickers

What was used:
- Markers
- Ruler
- Stickers

46

What was used:
- Die-cuts
- Stickers

What was used:
- Decorative ruler
- Die-cut
- Marker
- Stickers

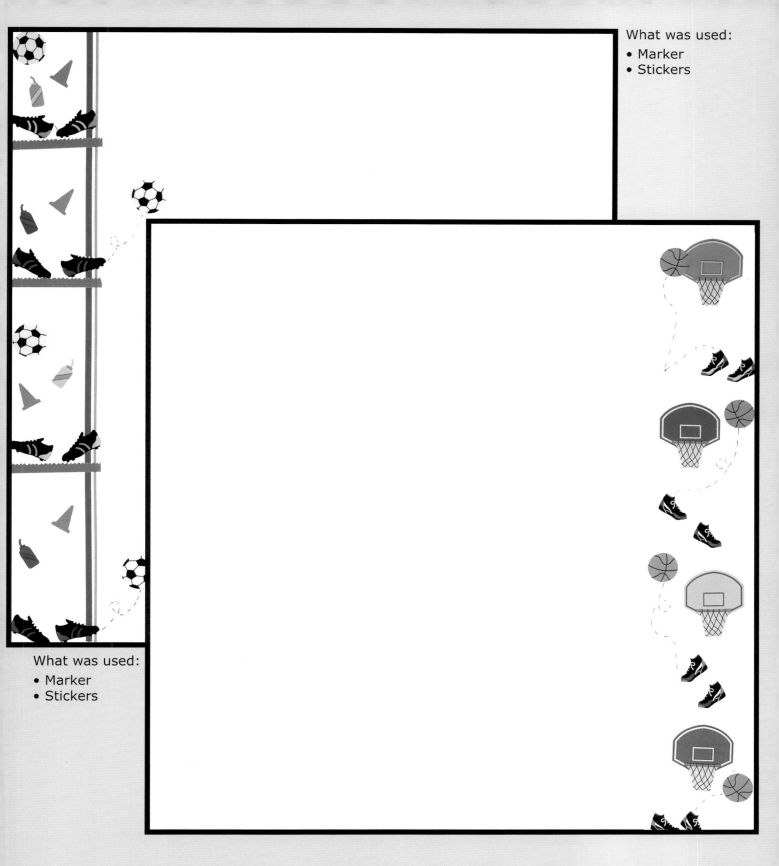

What was used:
• Marker
• Stickers

What was used:
• Marker
• Stickers

What was used:
- Markers
- Ruler
- Stickers

What was used:
- Die-cuts
- Stickers

DEC. 16. 1996

"MERRY MERRY CHRISTMAS"

DANCE

What was used:
- Decorative ruler
- Marker
- Stickers

What was used:
• Marker
• Stickers

What was used:
• Decorative ruler
• Markers
• Stickers

ON THE GO

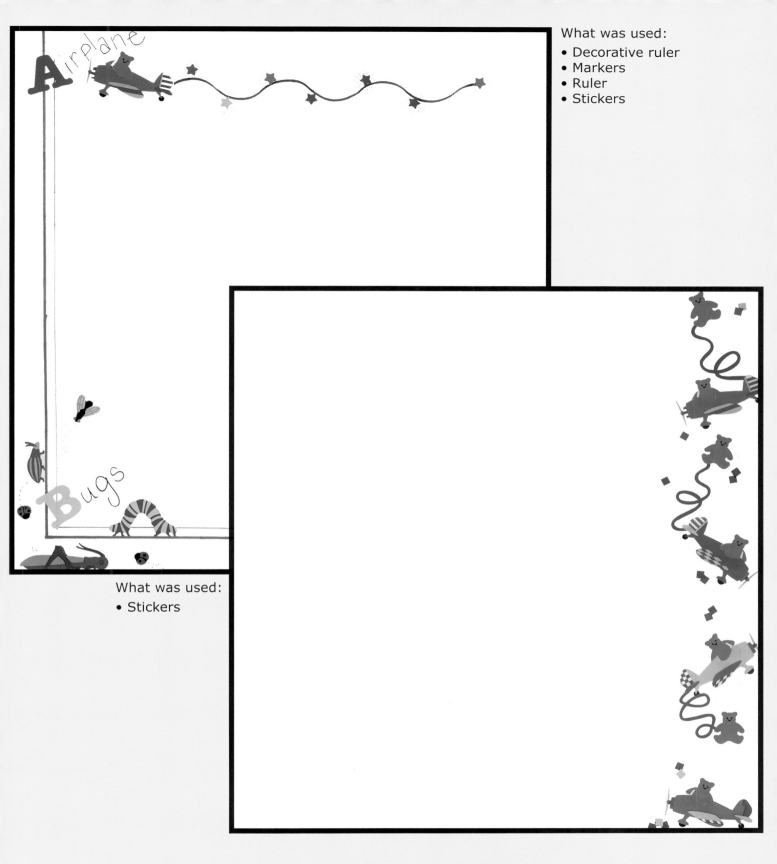

What was used:
- Decorative ruler
- Markers
- Ruler
- Stickers

What was used:
- Stickers

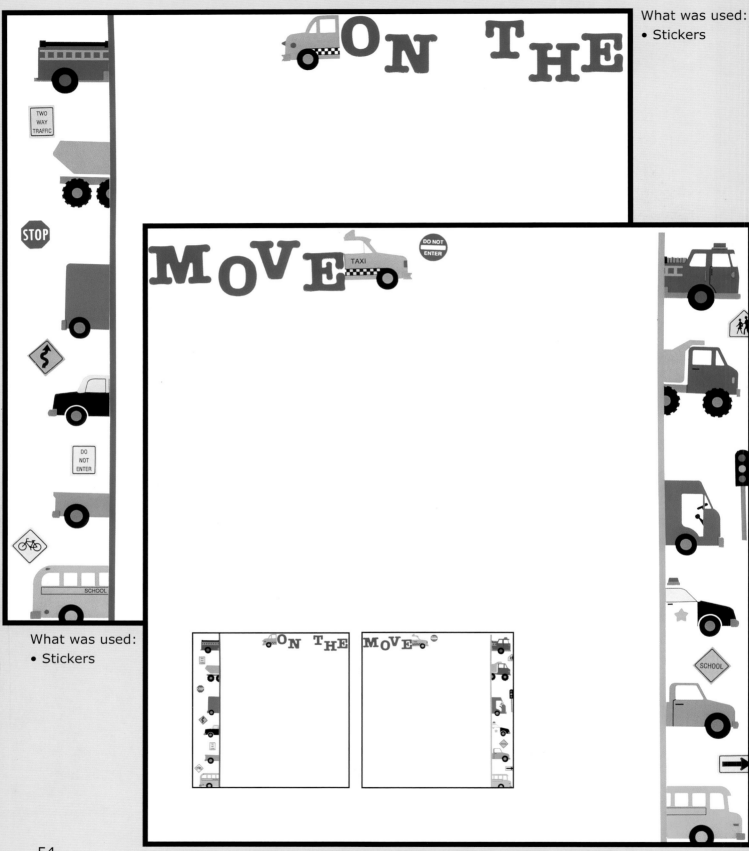

ON THE

MOVE

ON THE

MOVE

What was used:

- Die-cuts
- Strip of card stock
- Strip of patterned paper

Snips and snails
and puppy dog tails...

...That's what little boys are made of.

What was used:
- Decorative ruler
- Markers
- Stickers

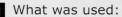

What was used:
• Stickers

What was used:
• Stickers

What was used:
• Marker
• Stickers

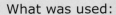

What was used:
• Stickers

58

What was used:
- Stickers
- Strip of card stock

What was used:
- Markers
- Stickers

What was used:
- Marker
- Stickers

What was used:
- Stickers
- Strip of card stock

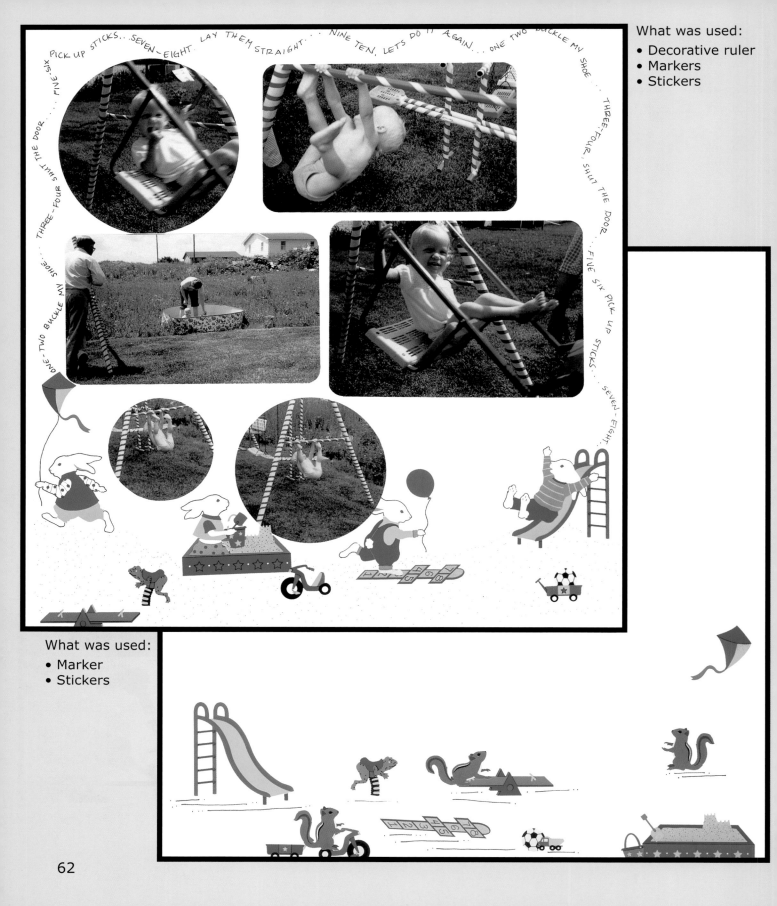

What was used:
- Marker
- Stickers

62

Happy Birthday

What was used:
• Stickers

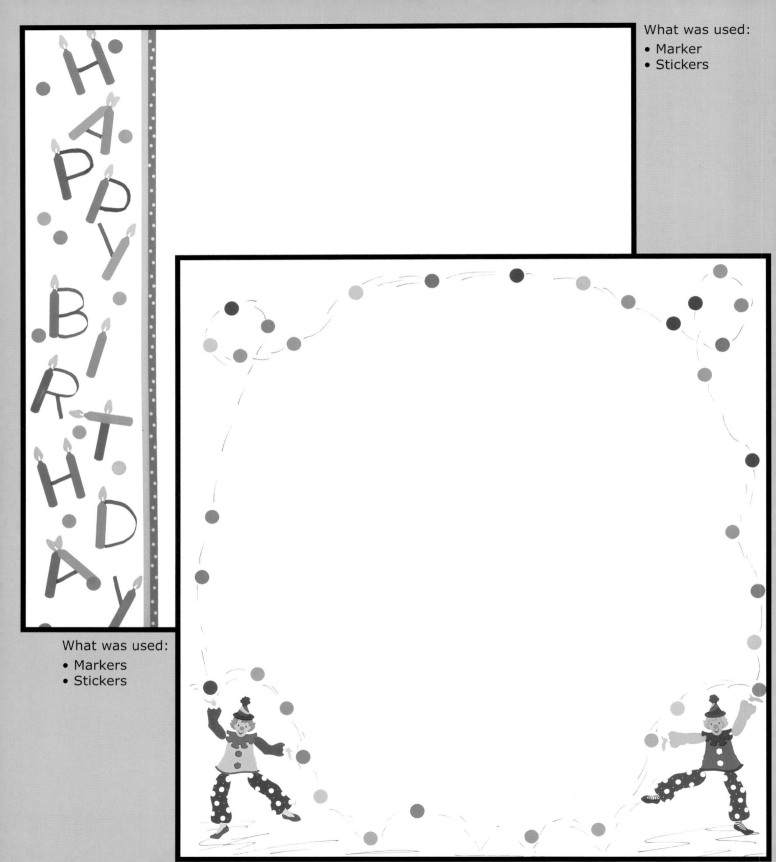

What was used:
• Marker
• Stickers

What was used:
• Markers
• Stickers

What was used:
- Die-cuts
- Stickers

What was used:
- Decorative ruler
- Marker
- Stickers

HAPPY BIRTHDAY

GRANDMA & GRANDPA BOEHME GAVE ASHLIE AND TAYLOR A BASKETBALL STANDING

ASHLIE, TANA BOEHME

WE CELEBRATED ASHLIE'S BIRTHDAY THREE TIMES

FIRST AT GRANDMA BOEHME'S HOUSE....

...SECOND AT EASTER AT UNCLE JIM'S HOUSE

MARCH 28, '97

MAR. 30

What was used:
- Markers
- Stickers

66

A TRUCKLOAD of FUN

What was used:

- Decorative ruler
- Die-cut
- Marker
- Stickers

Family Fun

What was used:
- Circle of card stock
- Stickers

What was used:
- Decorative ruler
- Markers
- Stickers

MARSHMALLOWS ROASTING
FIRE LIGHT
FISHERMEN BOASTING
STARRY NIGHTS
LET'S GO CAMPING!
LET'S GO CAMPING

What was used:
- Marker
- Stickers

FISH ON

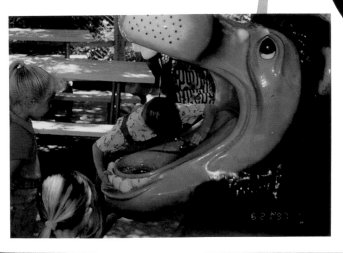

WHITNEY, ASHLIE, MOM, TORY

HOGLE

What was used:
- Die-cuts
- Marker
- Ruler
- Stickers

Utah's
HOGLE ZOO

brings you

FIELDTRIP WITH 1ST GRADERS   MAY 21, 1997

What was used:
- Die-cuts
- Marker
- Ruler
- Stickers

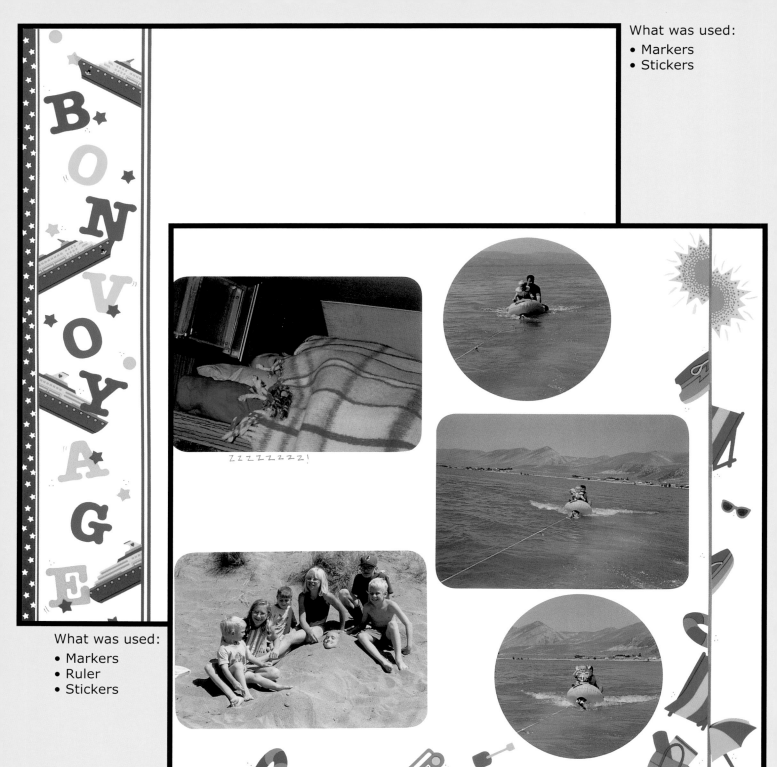

BON VOYAGE

Zzzzzzzz!

Bear Lake Aug. 1996

What was used:
• Markers
• Ruler
• Stickers

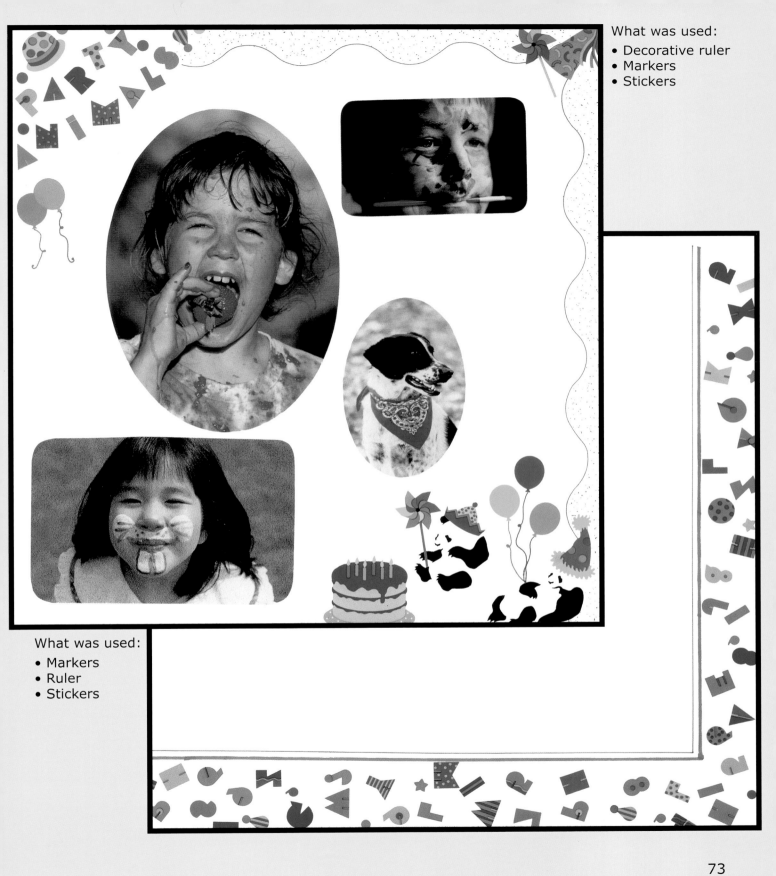

What was used:
- Markers
- Ruler
- Stickers

4th of July

SWIMMING
JULY 1-12
1996

DAD   TAYLOR   GRANDMA B.H.

DAD

SHADOW DANCIN'! ASHLIE   TAYLOR

PAINTING FROM CHERRY DAYS IN N...

TAYLOR TOOK THE PARENT-TOT CLASS. DAD TOOK A DAY OFF WORK TO GIVE MOM A BREAK.

TAYLOR ASALIE.

GOT AN ITCH?

FLOATING

HUMPTY DUMPTY HAD...

A GREAT FAL...

What was used:
- Marker
- Ruler
- Stickers

74

What was used:
- Markers
- Ruler
- Stickers

What was used:
- Die-cut
- Marker
- Stickers

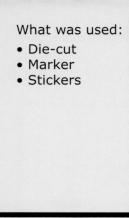

What was used:
- Marker
- Stickers

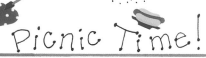

Picnic Time!

GRANDPA'S FARM

Vacation

MIAMI
MAY 1996
FLORIDA

What was used:
- Die-cuts
- Stickers

What was used:
- Stickers

What was used:
- Markers
- Ruler
- Stickers

What was used:
- Stickers

Best Dad in the World

What was used:
- Decorative ruler
- Die-cut
- Markers
- Ruler
- Stickers

What was used:
- Die-cuts
- Stickers

What was used:

- Die-cuts
- Markers
- Stickers

A FLOAT PLANE LANDING ON THE WATER WHILE WE WATCHED FROM THE BOAT.

SCOTT WAS IN MEETINGS SO I TOOK THE CRUISE ALONE.

HARD ROCK CAFE.

A CRUISE OF THE STARS HOUSES.

What was used:
- Marker
- Stickers

SEA WORLD

What was used:
- Die-cuts
- Stickers

SPLASH

What was used:
- Stickers

What was used:
- Card stock
- Patterned paper
- Stickers

What was used:
- Die-cuts
- Marker
- Stickers

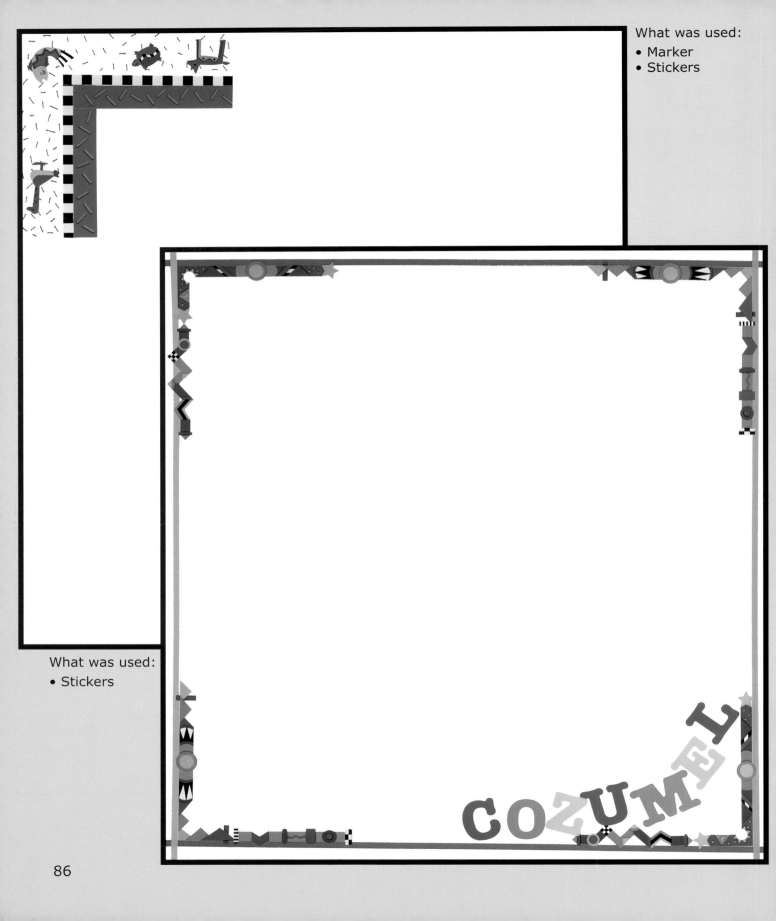

What was used:
- Marker
- Stickers

What was used:
- Stickers

COZUMEL

ARIZONA

What was used:
• Stickers

BAL HA

What was used:
- Die-cuts
- Marker
- Stickers

RBOUR

ITT Sheraton

What was used:
- Die-cuts
- Marker
- Stickers

Holidays & Seasons

What was used:
• Markers
• Stickers

What was used:
• Stickers

What was used:
• Markers
• Stickers

What was used:
- Decorative ruler
- Markers
- Ruler
- Stickers

VALENTINES

BE MINE DAY

92

HATS OFF!!

What was used:
- Decorative ruler
- Die-cuts
- Markers
- Ruler
- Stickers

What was used:
- Stickers

I ❤ DO!

What was used:
- Die-cut
- Stickers

What was used:
- Stickers

LUCKY DAY

UP UP & AWAY

What was used:
• Die-cuts
• Marker
• Stickers

SPRING HAS

SPRUNG

What was used:
• Marker
• Stickers

WHAT A TWEETHEART!

What was used:
• Marker
• Stickers

What was used:
• Marker
• Stickers

MY SUNSHINE

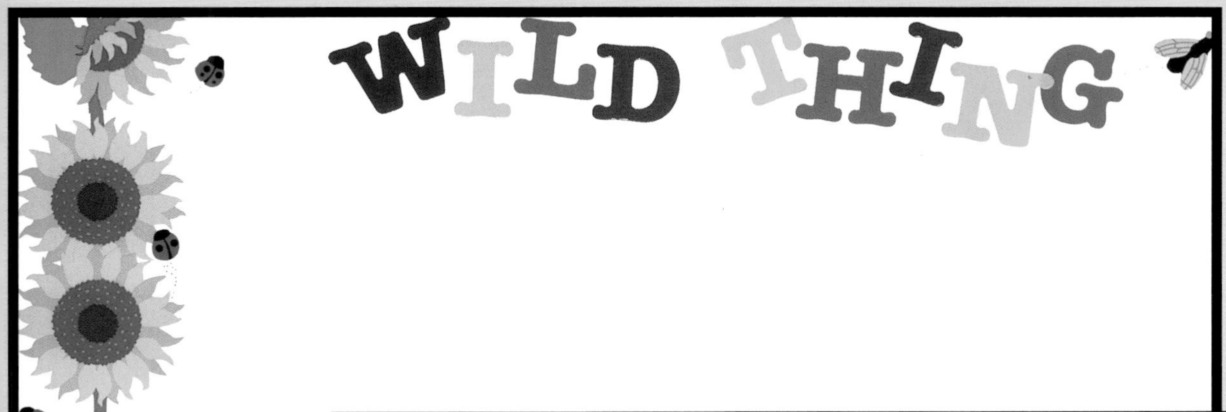
WILD THING

What was used:

- Die-cut
- Marker
- Stickers

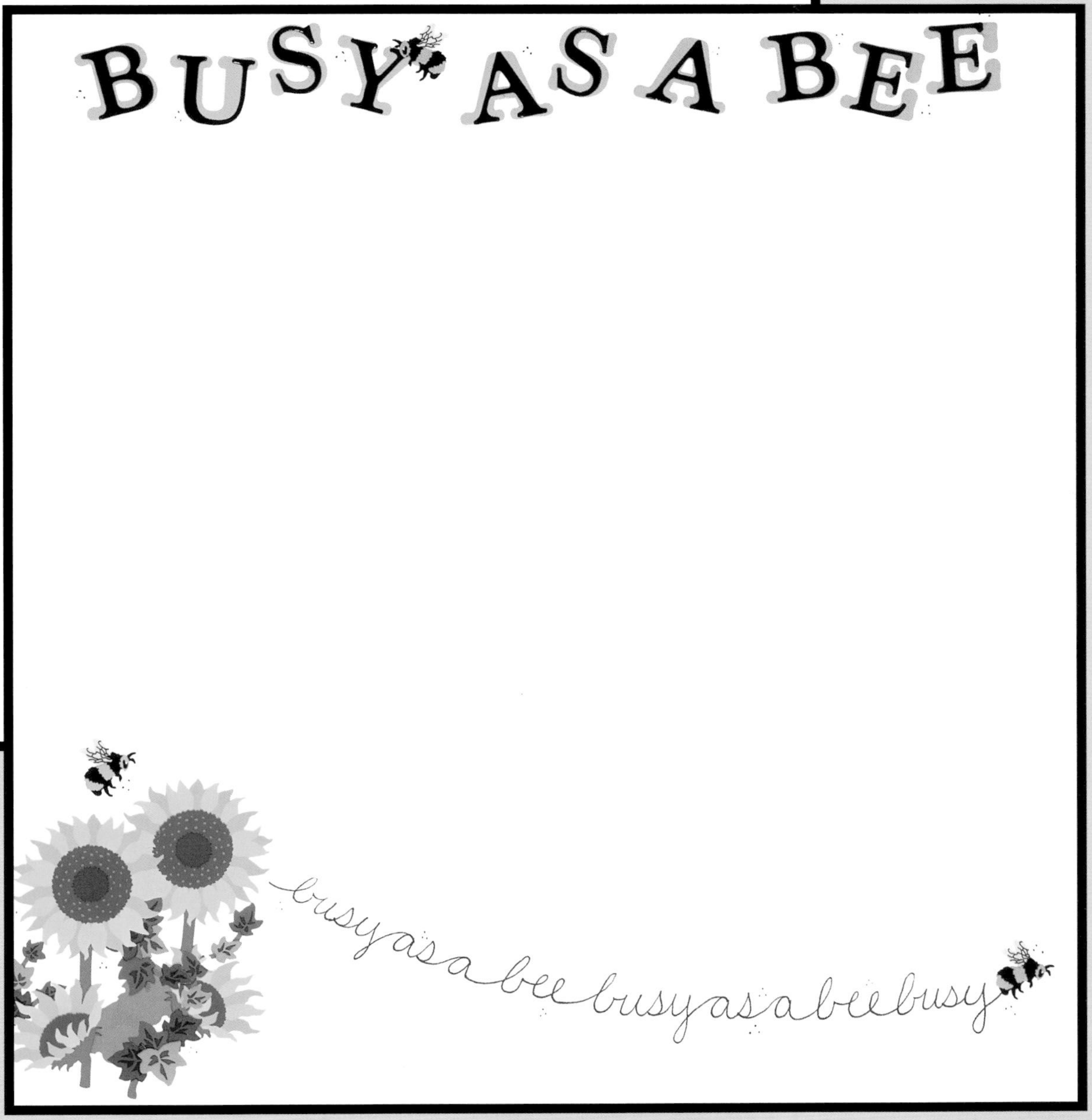
BUSY AS A BEE
busy as a bee busy as a bee busy

What was used:

- Marker
- Stickers

Ashlie   Taylor

Bunny holding lessons.

Delay action Birthday Prizes

A real Easter Bunny!

Mom

Taylor
Derek
(Bunny)

APRIL 7, 1996

Easter fun Hunt on empty lot for fun Prizes.

Easter Feasters.

EASTER
1996

Uncle Steve, aunt Kay
Allen

Aunt stacey uncle Jim
Redford

Dad

Grandma Barbara

Hippity Hoppity EASTER'S on it's way!

What was used:
• Decorative ruler
• Markers
• Stickers

98

Mom helped at Ashlie's school for her Easter Party... Taylor Too.

Taylor is Sierra Cragun's Partner for 3 legged race.

Easter Egg hunt at Lomond View Elementary

Bunny Basket Decor

Here comes Peter Cottontail... hoppin' down the...

see my Pretty egg!

Bunny Trail

Bunny ear Basket.

Hello My Name PETER

What was used:
- Decorative ruler
- Markers
- Square of card stock
- Stickers

EASTER·EGG·HUNT

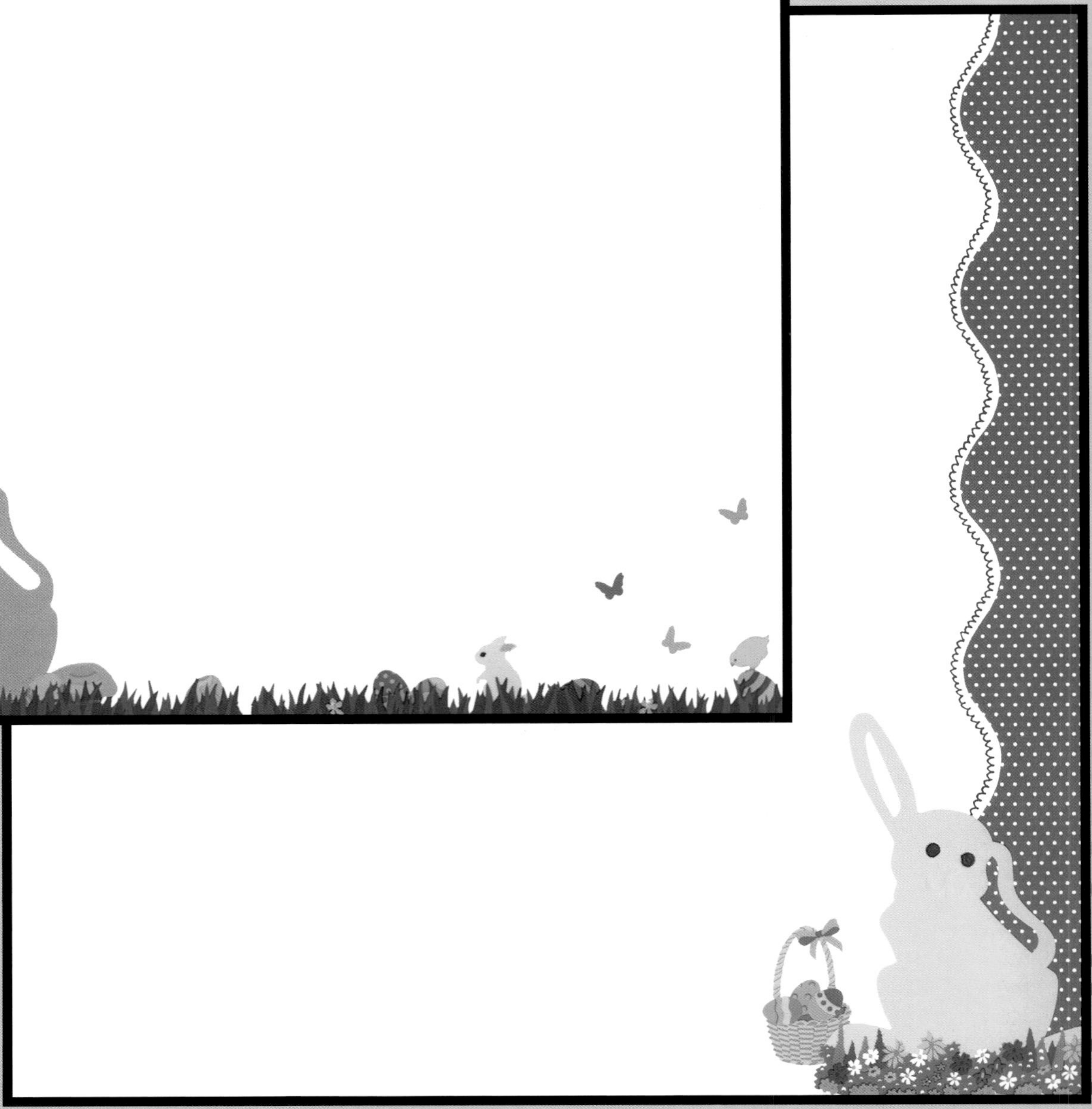

What was used:
- Decorative ruler
- Die-cut
- Stickers
- Strip of card stock

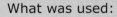

MOM HELPED THE KINDERGARTEN WITH THEIR EASTER PARTY. SHE WAS THE ROOM MOTHER HELPER. WE PLAYED GAMES HEARD A STORY AND DECORATED COOKIES TAYLOR CAME TOO!

TAYLOR BOEHME, SIERRA CRAGUN

ASHLIE BOEHME

EASTER

TWO EGGS PER BUNNY!

GRANDMA PREPARING EASTER DINNER

ASHLIE FINDING EGGS

What was used:
• Stickers

What was used:
- Die-cut
- Marker
- Stickers
- Strips of card stock

What was used:
- Stickers

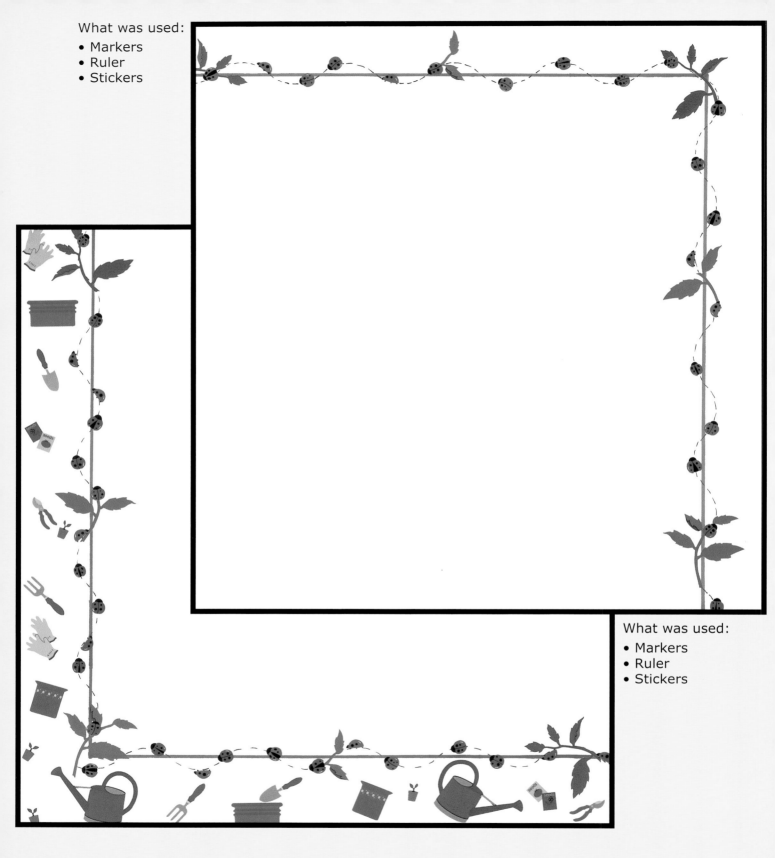

What was used:
- Markers
- Ruler
- Stickers

What was used:
- Markers
- Ruler
- Stickers

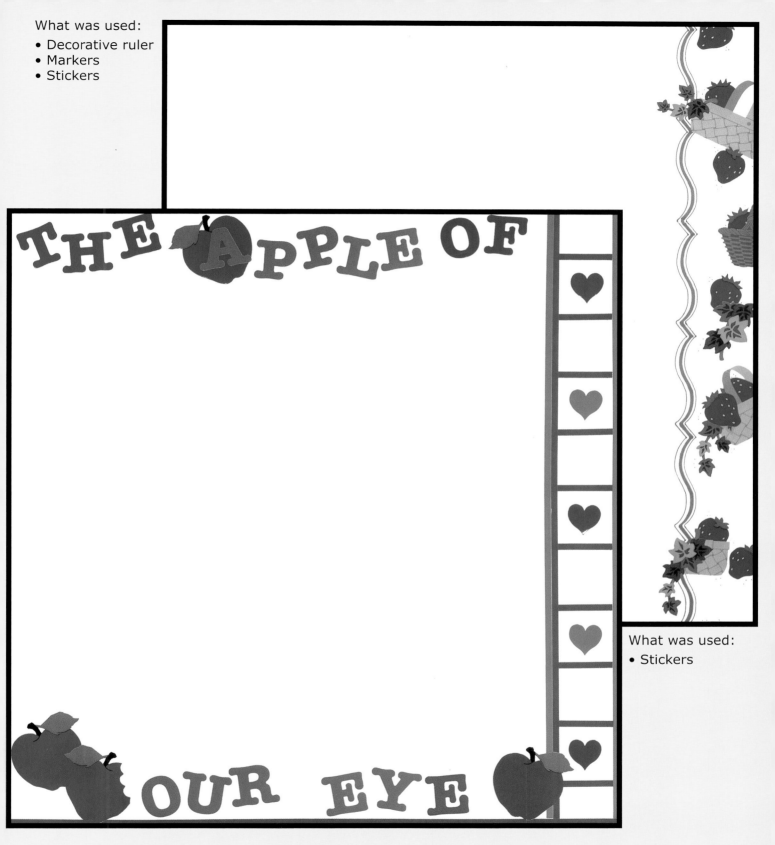

What was used:
- Decorative ruler
- Markers
- Stickers

THE APPLE OF OUR EYE

What was used:
- Stickers

What was used:
• Stickers

What was used:
• Stickers
• Strip of card stock

106

What was used:
• Stickers

Double Bubble, Toil and Trouble

What was used:
• Die-cut
• Markers
• Stickers

PUNKIN' PATCH

What was used:
- Die-cut
- Stickers

Joey's 1st Halloween

Our Little Pumpkin!

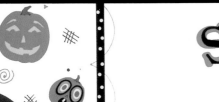

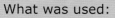

What was used:
- Decorative ruler
- Markers
- Stickers

What was used:
- Stickers

CHILL DUDE

COOL SUMMER FUN

SNOW FUN

What was used:
• Marker
• Stickers

What was used:
• Die-cuts
• Stickers

113

Not a creature was stirring . . . not even a mouse; ♥ The stockings were hung by the chimney with care in hopes that St. Nicholas soon would be there.

Not all through the house, When all through the house, When all through Christmas, 'Twas the night before Christmas,

We had a small Christmas party with Aunt Kay and her family and Uncle Jim and his family and Grandma.

opening a present from aunt Kay and uncle Steve

Dec. 14, 1996

what! Jim forgot?

Airplane ride with Grandma Barbara, Ashlie Taylor and dad. This was Taylor's first ride in a Cessna 172. He had been asking Dad to take him for a long time. Grandma said he had to hold her hand the whole ride but he seemed to enjoy it.

Grandma brought beads to string for grandchildren.

NEWGATE 4
FLY AWAY HOME 4
20   12-24 TUE
NEWGATE MOVIES 4
59486   15371272
$1.00

We went to a show early Christmas eve day with Grandma Barbara.

Mom's family always got to open one present on Christmas Eve. So we carried on the tradition this year by opening brand new home-made pajamas!

114

What was used:
• Marker
• Stickers

What was used:
• Stickers

What was used:
• Die-cuts
• Stickers
• Strip of
  patterned paper

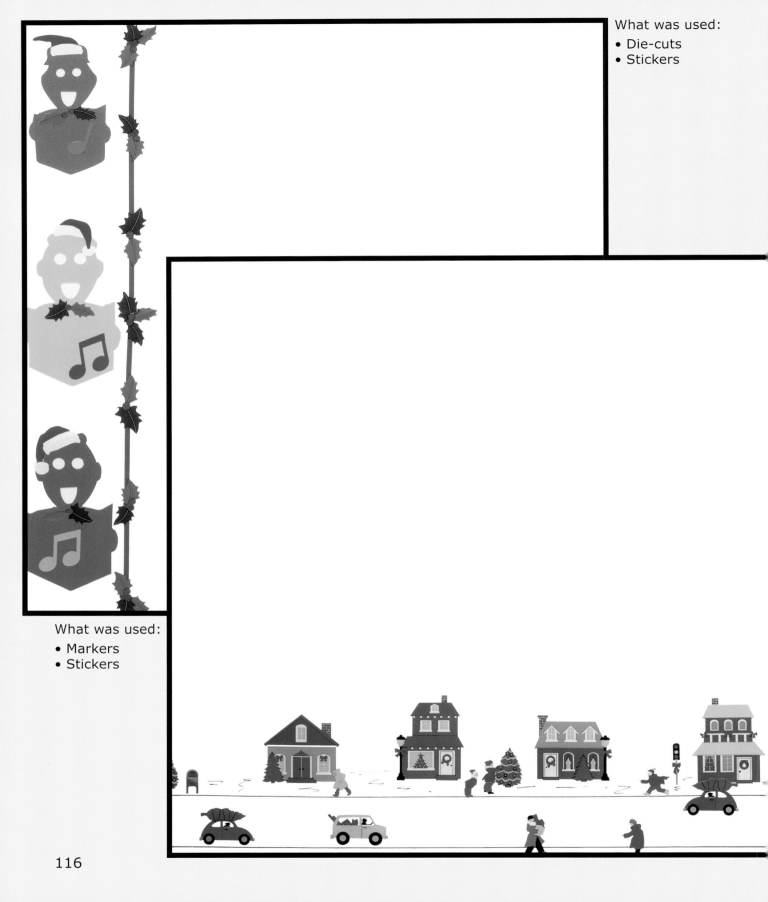

What was used:
• Die-cuts
• Stickers

What was used:
• Markers
• Stickers

Shelby adds
the finishing touch
to our Christmas tree!

Christmas
1999

What was used:
- Markers
- Stickers

What was used:
- Marker
- Stickers

NORTH POLE

What was used:
- Marker
- Stickers

What was used:
- Markers
- Ruler
- Stickers

What was used:
- Stickers

What was used:
- Decorative ruler
- Markers
- Stickers

WE WISH YOU A MERRY CHRIS "MESS".... AND A HAPPY NEW YEAR!!

Dear Santa,

I want a baby doll and a stroller for Christmas. Please bring baby brother a cow that goes moo.

Thank you, Santa!

I love you, Carly

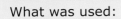
What was used:
- Decorative ruler
- Markers
- Stickers

What was used:
- Die-cut
- Stickers

No Season No Reason

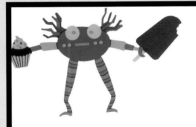

What was used:
- Marker
- Stickers

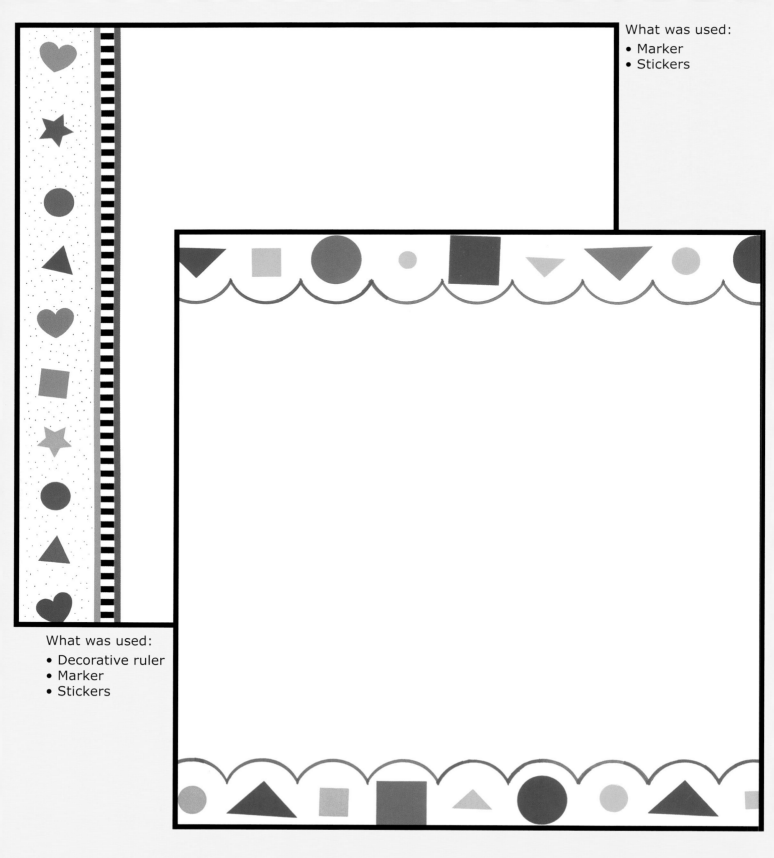

What was used:
• Marker
• Stickers

What was used:
• Decorative ruler
• Marker
• Stickers

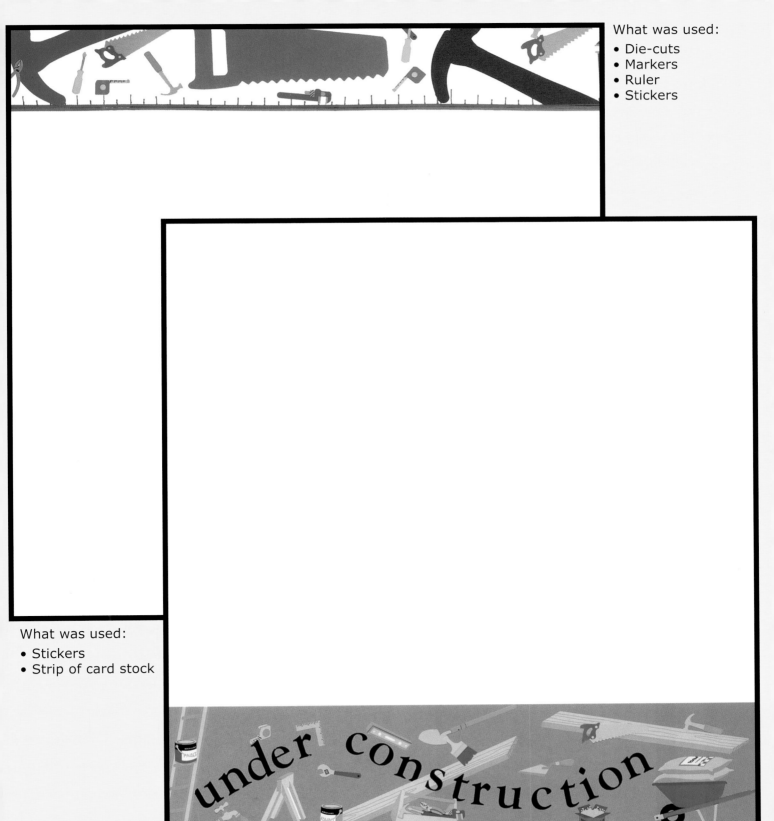

What was used:
• Die-cuts
• Markers
• Ruler
• Stickers

What was used:
• Stickers
• Strip of card stock

under construction

ONE IN A MILLION

THE DIFFERENCE BETWEEN THE MEN AND THE BOYS, IS THE PRICE OF THEIR TOYS!

What was used:
• Stickers
• Strip of card stock

SUPER

STAR

What was used:
• Marker
• Ruler
• Stickers

127

Index

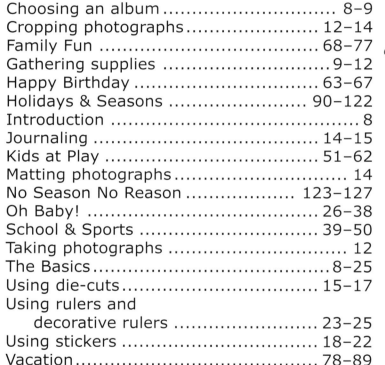